Life After Leaving

My Amish World

Eirene Eicher

Dedication and Acknowledgements:

To my seven sons, daughters-in-law, and grandchildren whom I love more than life.
To my dear mother and siblings, I say a thank you in your role in helping me become who I am today.
To my many supportive friends and fans who have encouraged me throughout my writing journey, beginning with my first book called Leaving my Amish World. And now book 2, Life After Leaving my Amish World.

I can't say thank you enough to Ashley Emma. She has been a huge support in helping me with all the behind the scenes work that goes into publishing and launching a book. She is an expert and I so appreciate her help, her expertise and her willingness to help me when I get stuck.
Lastly a big thank you to Rebecca Strong for your willingness to guide me through word doc and for all of your time and effort.
Without all of you this would not be possible. I am eternally grateful for all of you. Thank you.

www.EireneEicher.com

Authors note:

Because of the nature of this story and everyone involved, names and places have been changed for the protection of everyone involved. My intent is not to hurt anyone but to bring awareness to someone who, like me, may be struggling or "stuck" in life and who could learn there is help available and find the courage to reach out, or to prevent another young mother from all the pain I've endured all these years.

Also please keep in mind all Amish communities have different customs and rules, and some in this book may not be what you are familiar with.

Other than the name changes and the place changes, this is my 100% true story.

***

All bible verses are from the King James Version Bible.

***

You can contact me at eicherirene7@gmail.com

Table Of Contents

Chapter 1

Life After Leaving my Amish World

Growing up in the Amish faith was most enjoyable. I loved the simple, quiet life without all the technology and the fast-paced environment of the modern world today, but it does have its drawbacks, such as limited education and lack of knowledge of the outside world.

Leaving the safety and security of our controlled culture was frightening to say the least. Launching out into a whole new world that I knew nothing about and taking my boys away from the only world they'd ever known and into the unknown world was going to be a challenge. Leaving my Amish world was excruciatingly painful. It was a tough decision, but I had to think of my little boys and their future. I wanted so much more for them then what I was given. I wanted them to grow up and have an education and be able to make healthy decisions and become strong individuals. I wanted each one of them to become their own true selves and be taught to follow their hearts and become who they truly were meant to be. I hoped and prayed they would make healthy choices and realize their full potential. I knew I had to rely on my God to lead, guide and direct me.

I want to give my readers a brief recap of my first book, *Leaving My Amish World*, where I talk about having been born and raised Old Order Amish. Being born into a family of 14 children, with me being the oldest daughter and having twin brothers one year older than me, was a fun adventure as well as a lot of work. We worked hard and played hard. We were taught the value of not only having good work ethic and also enjoy it. There was never a dull moment, no time to be bored. Being raised without all the tech toys and screens of today, we learned to be creative and were happy for free time after working hard. I enjoyed shooting baskets with my brothers, who were very competitive. I don't remember winning against them very often in a game of basketball (or "HORSE," as the game was called). But it was fun to try. Growing up in a family of mostly boys, I became a tomboy.

My mom used to threaten to make me a denim dress, since girls and women who are raised Amish don't wear pants.

That didn't stop me from following my two oldest brothers up into the hayloft and climbing up onto the barn roof. So much more exciting than baking a cake, making noodles, washing dishes, or doing mountains of laundry, which was a never-ending job in itself. One day in particular my brothers were being their ornery selves—being twins, they were double trouble—and on this day my dad and his crew of workers were standing in a group talking while I followed my brothers up the ladder to the barn roof. All of a sudden a gust of wind blew the skirt of my dress up over my head, showing my underwear-covered bottom. I was so embarrassed. I never heard the end of that, and I was thinking that maybe my mom should follow through with her threat of making me a denim dress.

One of my favorite things to do was horseback riding. I absolutely *loved* it. Nothing compares to the thrill and excitement of riding a horse full-stretch gallop through an open field. I never took lessons—I learned from my family. I'll never forget the thrill of the speed, the feeling of freedom with the wind in my face, or the smell of the green grass along with the leather saddle I was clinging to. I absolutely loved that experience.

I loved horses for as long as I can remember. We depended on them for transportation as well as entertainment. My grandpa had teams of huge, heavy workhorses. It was impressive how powerful they seemed to me as I watched my uncles hitch them to the farm equipment using four horses to a plow to work the fields. Those are some wonderful memories. I'd love for my kids and grandkids to experience some of them.

More cherished memories are of friends who would bring their riding horses to our cookouts that my dad hosted. Those were the good ole days, I guess you could say. We sure did enjoy them. My dad grilled the meat or roasted a hog, and my mom would cook a huge feast. Dad's friends would bring their musical instruments, and my sisters and I would sing and yodel. They even brought their horses for us to ride.

My older twin brothers had ponies that were also twins. At these cookouts they would race the ponies and do some barrel jumping and harness racing. It was a fun time. They named the ponies after two of our aunts, Rosie and Sylvie. And just like my brothers, the ponies were difficult to tell apart. They were just as competitive as my brothers, which made it double the fun!

These are only a few of the precious memories I have of my childhood and life of growing up in an Amish home. I loved my life and never thought I would ever leave. The thought never even crossed my mind until after I grew up and married Mark. That's when life became such that I was forced to seek God for answers.

As a very young seventeen-year-old bride, pregnant with our first child, I began to experience life with an alcoholic husband along with all the problems and uncertainties that come with alcoholism. I didn't know anything about the disease when I got married. Back then we all drank alcohol. It was just what we did. In my mind, an alcoholic was a drunk passed out in an alley somewhere. Someone who could not function in society.

But I would soon learn all about the disease of alcoholism and how it really is a family disease. I learned that people like me really are enablers and are very codependent. I soon learned it would be a very hard struggle, and it drove me to my knees in search of answers and solutions for me and my family.

3

Chapter 2

There seemed to be no way out. In our culture I was taught that no matter what my husband did or how abusive he became, I had to stay with him. Divorce was never an option. It was until death do us part. There would be many, many times when I felt like I could not go on another day. Painful times when I felt so alone in the world. So unloved and ugly and unlovable.

It was after Mark was arrested and taken to jail for drinking and driving without a license that the Amish church decided to excommunicate both Mark and me. Since we lived right across the road from my parents and them having to shun us, it became way too painful for them and us too, and so we decided to move out of our neighborhood and begin a new life outside of the Amish community. We thought this was the best decision for us and our sons.

We moved ourselves and our five boys into a one-bedroom apartment in town. Imagine that! Seven people in a tiny one-bedroom apartment with no communication with the rest of our world. We had no money or phone, and neither one of us had a driver's license.

We had no transportation since we couldn't keep a horse and buggy in town. It was absolutely devastating. My husband looked at me and said, "Just look what you got us into!"

At that moment I believed that it was all my fault. Whenever Mark pointed his finger and placed the blame on me, I believed him. But later after lots of counseling I realized it was Marks fault, it was his actions not mine that got us kicked out of the Amish church. I asked myself the same question though. What did I get us into? It was one of the most devastating moments of my life. I threw myself across the bed and sobbed my heart out.

Where would we go from here? How would we pick up the pieces of this broken, shattered world of ours? How would we survive financially? All 10 of Marks Amish employees had quit working because Mark now had to be shunned by them. Life seemed hopeless at this moment.

We left everything we had ever known—our whole world, friends, family, and acquaintances—and ventured out into a new, uncharted territory. And we just did not know how to do this. How does a person start a new life with so little? There was very little to work with.

I walked uptown to the pay phone, dropped in a quarter and called my friend Sharon. She was my anchor. My lifeline. My guidance. Where would I be without her?

Since Mark had been charged with multiple offenses, including driving without a license, the courts ordered him to go to alcohol counseling for a whole year. He would not be able to get his driver's license until this was completed since he had been caught driving illegally without a license.

"Truly all things work together for good to those who love the Lord and are called according to His purpose" (Romans 8:28).

This whole thing was a blessing in disguise. Maybe, just maybe, Mark would get help with his alcohol addiction through the mandatory counseling and AA. At least he would be forced to stay sober for a year.

Sharon came over one day and said, "You need to drive my car. Practice your driving and parking so that you can go get your driver's license." And so I did. She then took me to the license branch, where I passed the written and driver's exam. How thrilled and excited I was! I felt liberated. Now I needed a car. How was all this going to happen? I once again took it to the Lord, and once again He provided for me.

Mark and I went with the neighbors to purchase a used car—an Oldsmobile. I finally had my license and a car! My very own transportation. It was a feeling of relief, liberation and hope. Later that night I was taking my babysitter home. She had stayed with the five little boys while we purchased the car. It was a very dark night, and I was traveling on Highway 27 going out of Geneva when all of a sudden, the motor of the car shut off and the lights went out! What a scary feeling! I guided the car as it coasted off to the side of the road and prayed for a police officer. When I looked in my rearview mirror I saw flashing lights coming toward me. I was never so relieved to see a police car behind me. The officers were very nice. They called the tow truck for me and took my babysitter to her house and dropped her off. On the way back to my house I told them I might just have to go back to driving a horse and buggy. We all chuckled at the thought.

Mark decided to hire a non-Amish employee and started back to work. No crew. Just the two of them, which brought in some desperately needed funds. It helped that he couldn't drink. That really helped a lot. He was forced to stay sober and face reality. He needed to realize that not everything that went wrong was my fault. He needed to stop shifting the blame onto my shoulders and start being accountable. I needed to stop accepting the blame and enabling him. This was hard. It was all new to me. I didn't realize how very dysfunctional we really were.

During this excruciating and difficult time in my life, God became very real to me. I literally had to rely on Him for everything, and so I did. He never failed me. He was always close by my side. I relied heavily on His Word, and that is where I found strength, wisdom and guidance. I would read and pray, in sweet communion with God. He felt so close to me during those turbulent times. He was and still is a very present help in time of trouble. Many times I would pray His Word back to Him. He became my very close companion, and I couldn't imagine life without Him. I also leaned very heavily on my best friend, Sharon, who was more like a mom and mentor than a friend. She taught me so much and was a source of great comfort. She was actually the one to give my boys their very first non-Amish haircut. Wow! What a change! We hadn't even had a chance to buy their first non-Amish clothes. So many changes in such a short time. It was very mind-boggling.

At this point we had five young boys, who had no clue about what was happening. The two oldest were in school during this transition and had to endure the pain of rejection and ridicule from both the Amish and non-Amish kids in school. The Amish kids no longer wanted to be friends because they dressed differently, and the non-Amish kids called them names such as "half breeds" among other cruel actions and words being hurled at them. My heart bled for them. They were confused and did not understand why their world was being turned upside down. I knew this would be a painful time in their lives, but I also knew the time would come when they would understand and be happy about this change, however painful it might be at this time.

Chapter 3

Trying to figure out how to fit into a whole new world that I knew nothing about was more than a challenge. I had to learn how to change everything from dressing my children and myself to the way I cooked, cleaned, and bathed. No longer did I need to carry in every drop of water I used. I now had running water and modern conveniences. I now had a gas stove, a microwave, and a dishwasher. Even the way I cleaned the house and swept the floors changed. I could now plug in a sweeper and vacuum my floors. I could now walk on carpets.

I felt liberated in many ways and lost in others. I felt liberated in the areas of modern conveniences and no longer having to hitch up the horse and buggy to go get my groceries. But I felt lost in the areas of trying to figure out direction in life and how to cope without my extended family. How could I live life without having regular visits with my sisters and my mom? How were my little boys going to cope without their cousins? There is no replacement for family and blood relatives. How painful it was for these little boys to also feel the stings of rejection.

Sebastian, my oldest, was so crushed when he went to sit on grandpa's lap like he always did in the past and he was rejected. Grandpa no longer played hide-and-seek with the boys. The look of confusion on their faces was almost more than I could bear. They didn't understand what was happening. How do you help little children understand these ridiculous rules of shunning when we as adults didn't even understand them? If only we could all live in the freedom that God intended for us. The very reason He sent His son, Jesus, to die on the cross for us—to do away with the laws and legalism. Oh my. The great deception of religion versus true Christianity. Freedom in Christ.

How this would all work out, I did not know. One thing I knew for sure: God would never ask me to do more than I could bear. It was extremely hard for my little boys to understand the transition and the shunning, or "rejection," which is what it equates to emotionally. There would be many, many times in the years ahead that my boys would see the shunning and the rejection. It was just too painful for them to even be around and interact with our Amish relatives. Shunning is one thing I do not understand; I never have, and I never will. I have never seen in the Bible where Jesus did this to people. He sat with the sinners, ate with them, and loved on them. That love is the drawing power, not rejection. Shunning is a form of judging, which the Bible speaks strongly against. In fact in 1Peter 4:8 it reads, And above all things have fervent charity among yourselves: for charity shall cover the multitude of sins.

We lived in the apartment for only a couple of months when we found a house in the country for rent. It was somewhat outside our Amish community, giving us a much-needed fresh start. The boys would be starting school in a non-Amish environment. A fresh start without the shunning.

The house we moved into was nothing fancy, but with some paint, new carpet and a good cleaning, it became home to us. A new beginning in a new world! We had a lot to learn as we made our way into a totally new world, we knew very little about.

This was a venture I never would have attempted on my own. Instead, I was led by my Lord and Savior. He made a way where there was no way. There would be many, many times when I would see the hand of God at work in our lives, from little things like the time I rented a carpet shampooer from the store in a town approximately 20 minutes away. I had never shampooed a carpet before, since this modern way of living was all new to me, and so after I had finished cleaning the bedroom carpet, I went to turn on the machine to clean the second bedroom, but it would not turn on. What? I had broken the machine? Now what? There was no way in this world I could afford to buy a new one to replace it, and I didn't want to take it back broken. Oh, dear! What was I to do? It was just me with three babies at home. The two oldest boys were in school. Mark was at work. I was in a predicament.

So, I did what I always do and took it to my Lord. I asked Him to show me what to do. Suddenly I had a bright idea! What if I could take the starter switch out and find a replacement? Hmmm. That might work! I went out to the garage and found the proper tools. As I took the screws out of the machine, I knew I was taking a huge chance. I might have just broken it permanently. It was a chance I had to take.

After taking the starting mechanism out of the machine, I quickly gathered my three babies and drove the 20 minutes into town to the hardware store. They did not have the exact replacement but something similar. Ok, I would try it. As I hurried back home, I was hoping against hope this would work. What if? What if? What if this didn't work? But what if it did? I would certainly try my best. If it did work, it would spare me a huge bill to replace the whole machine.

Quickly I took the babies inside. Gave them snacks and settled them into their playtime routine and feverishly started to reassemble the starter into the shampooer. This just had to work. After I screwed in the last screw, holding my breath, I plugged the cord into the outlet and pushed the starter button. Lo and behold, it started right up! What a relief! Oh my goodness! What a sense of accomplishment. I cannot even express the gratitude I felt as I finished cleaning my carpets. I sailed through the rest of the afternoon on pure adrenaline after all that anxiety and excitement. My Lord did it again. He walked me through to a solution. The Scripture verse came alive to me again: "I can do all things through Christ, who strengthens me" (Philippians 4:13). Living here would give us a new beginning, and the boys would go to a country school where no one knew they had been Amish. They seemed to adapt fairly well to the new school and environment.

Chapter 4

Mark worked hard day in and day out. Finding good employees became a problem. He struggled with the work situation, and finding himself and his place in life in an unfamiliar world was extremely difficult. Life would be very trying at times, especially since we were not on the same page spiritually. While his way of dealing with the stresses of life included alcohol (way too much, I might add), I learned to turn to the one true God and His Word. His promises. This gave me much-needed peace and strength. Many times I would ask God for wisdom according to James 1:5, which says, "If any of you lack wisdom, let him ask of God, that giveth to all men liberally, and upbraideth not; and it shall be given him."

Mere words cannot express the love, joy and strength that comes from serving God. Hearing that still, small voice. Just knowing He has me covered and that He will provide for my every need. Knowing I can go to Him at any time of the day or night is a security that cannot be explained. This has gotten me through some really tough times.

The first few months of living out in the countryside away from the community gave us a reprieve, in a sense. The weekends were a time for the boys and their dad and me to bond and become closer, as now that was all we had. We had each other and tried to find our way into a new, unfamiliar world. The struggles were real! Often, I would think back to the time when we were first leaving the Amish. We had to start all over again, all by ourselves. No family to turn to. Mark did not want to go to church, so I established myself in a church in Fort Wayne, Indiana, where my best friend, Sharon, attended. Mark would go occasionally, but for the most part it was me and my five little boys. Taking them to church and teaching them about the Lord Jesus was of utmost importance to me. How I wished Mark would share that conviction with me.

I was ever so thankful for the help of my friend Sharon. I don't know where I would be if it had not been for her support. Many times, we would pray together over the struggles that we had. The church services were very long, and my boys got so tired of sitting in a church service for three hours. I've had my regrets about making them do this. I understand why they preferred to stay home with their dad instead of going to church with Mom.

The spiritual struggles were very real. It was excruciatingly painful to have lost the companionship of my siblings and parents. They live in a different world from mine now. And so, when I didn't have the spiritual support of my husband, it hurt even that much more. There are no words to describe the pain of rejection—aka "shunning"—from my family and friends when leaving the Amish Church. I tried my best to help them understand that I did not leave God's church but that He was leading me in a new direction, so I needed to leave in obedience to my Lord and Savior. It wasn't that I wanted to leave the only world I had ever known. I was simply obeying what God was asking me to do.

I did not understand how one man, Jakob Ammann, could start a church all the way back in 1693 and call it by his own name. the name Amish is taken from the name Ammann as in Jakob Ammann.

Jakob Ammann had a disagreement with a converted Catholic priest called Menno Simons, who started his own church, aka the Mennonites. Jakob Ammann decided to become stricter and incorporated the shunning. The Amish first began arriving in the USA back in the early to mid-1700s. They were attracted by the promise of Religious Freedom. Early Amish settled in Southeastern Pennsylvania. One of the original settlements that became the well-known community at Lancaster County.

I still do not understand why the Amish are so dedicated to one man's belief, when the Bible clearly teaches an independent, one-on-one relationship with God Himself. It is one thing for them to believe this, but to judge and condemn people who decide to follow the Bible's teaching was and still is beyond my comprehension. All this shunning and rejection causes unspeakable pain in the name of religion. This is totally opposite of what the Word describes as Christian attributes, or the fruits of the Holy Spirit: love, joy, peace, goodness, kindness, and gentleness (Galatians 5:22-23). How can it be that the emphasis is on the outward instead of focusing on God's Word and being filled with the Holy Spirit? The severance of our ties with all of our families was extremely painful.

Many times, I wondered if God would forgive me if I disobeyed Him to go back to be with family. As I entertained that thought, Matthew 10:37 came to mind: "He that loveth father or mother more than me is not worthy of me: and he that loveth son or daughter more than me is not worthy of me." I was also reminded of all the struggles that my Anabaptist forefathers went through to follow Christ. They literally gave their lives for Him. They were singing as they burned to death at the stake. They were happy to suffer for His name's sake. As my Lord and Savior Jesus Christ was judged and rejected. If He could do that for me, then surely, I can bear my cross for Him.

I was not the only one hurting from the loss of family ties; my husband was struggling too and so were my sweet, innocent little boys. They could not understand why they could no longer play with their cousins or visit with Grandma and Grandpa and aunts and uncles. How would I be able to explain this to them in a way that their young minds could understand? How could I tell them the reason we were being shunned was because we went to another church and no longer wore Amish clothes? It did not make sense to me. How was it going to make sense to them?

It was very difficult to leave our community. The struggle to adapt to a whole new world was indescribable. At times the pain was unbearable. Being alienated from my extended family is a kind of suffering I have yet to accurately describe. I haven't found the definition of such incredible hurt in Webster's dictionary. Of course, making new friends helped somewhat, but in my world, there is no replacement for family. I could no longer look forward to going to Mom's for the day to hang out with her and my sisters. This was the hardest of all. No more confiding in them or sharing my heart and life events or my daily struggles and victories. It helped tremendously that I could talk to my friend Sharon on a daily basis, sometimes several times a day. She must have had a God-given patience to be able to help me through the transition from one world into a whole new one.

Chapter 5

The struggle was real,not only was I struggling with my own decisions, but also not having the spiritual or emotional support from my husband and trying to keep a family united for the sake of my five little boys was almost impossible. This drove me to my knees in prayer to my one true God, where my strength came from. In Him all things are possible. Absolutely nothing is too hard for Him. I also relied on my favorite scripture, Romans 8:28: "We know that all things work together for good to them that love God, to them who are called according to his purpose." This promise always gave me great comfort.

Another source of comfort was the many new friends I made at church. They know who they are. These are the true friends more precious than diamonds. I love them still with all my heart. I looked to them as sisters and as examples to follow. They would love, accept and support me emotionally. That helped me more than they will ever know.

I want to mention my friend Sylvia, whom I looked up to and greatly appreciated and admired. It seemed to me that she had it all together and lived the American dream. She had a beautiful family and a nice home not far from me, she worked as a registered nurse! She always looked as if she had it all together. She is a gorgeous woman and loved the Lord just as I did. I wanted to be just like her (when I grew up). The thought of going back to school and becoming a nurse was a dream of mine, but first I wanted to raise my boys. I had a desire to raise them up in the way that they should go, according to the Word of God. No one would be able to take my place in their lives.

We still had our horse, Bess. We couldn't bear the thought of selling her just yet, even though by this time Mark and I both had our driver's licenses and each our own vehicles. We didn't have a need for a horse and buggy anymore. It was just that Bess had become a part of our family, and the boys still enjoyed climbing up on her back for a short jaunt and playing in the barn after feeding her. These were comforting, familiar activities they still enjoyed so much.

One Saturday afternoon Mark had taken the boys to the barbershop for haircuts. The barber there was highly recommended and worked from his home in the country. The boys and Mark felt very comfortable with him cutting their hair. This particular Saturday as he cut their hair, he told Mark about a home for sale not far from his house. Mark came home excited about going to check it out. We piled the boys into the van and drove the 15 minutes to the address that was given to Mark.

As we pulled into the driveway that was overgrown and barely visible, it was obvious the place wasn't cared for. The boys anxiously peeked out of the car windows at the old green house and said, "We don't want to live there!" It did look pretty unappealing, but Mark and I both saw potential. There was also a big wooden barn and a little chicken coop type building, and we both knew with a lot of hard work, cleaning and painting, the boys would love living there. It sat on an acre and a half, right across the road from a huge forest with lots of trees. This seemed like a perfect place to raise a family of all boys, with room for them to run and play. But this also meant that the boys would be back in the same school district they had attended while being Amish.

After a lot of consideration, we decided this was the right move. The boys were still young enough that they would be able to adapt to their new environment. And they would be surrounded by people they knew. I prayed many prayers for them to have good friends and not be bullied by the ones who were upset that they were no longer Amish. And so once again there were changes that all of us had to adapt to. It was times like this when we felt like we were alone on an island. We could no longer go to our Amish families for help since we were banned from the community. These were some excruciatingly painful times. I could no longer go to my parents or siblings for help since they believed that they had to shun us. I was extremely thankful for my friend Sharon and the emotional and spiritual support she provided.

Moving was a huge job, especially in the colder fall weather. With very little help, Mark and I packed up our belongings and moved into our new home the day we had possession of it. We were both taught to work hard as kids growing up, which served us well now in this time. We worked together as a team, and with the help of Mark's employee, we got most of our belongings moved in one day. Even our little guys pitched in, as kids do. With the truck loaded, we headed to the new house with the first of many loads. The kids were anxious to get to the place that they would call home until they grew up and ventured out into their own world. As we pulled into the driveway, they excitedly stumbled over each other, each wanting to be the first to run the property. They soon busied themselves with exploring the woods and the house and barn from top to bottom, making sure to see each nook and cranny. Their excitement grew as they realized the freedom and fun they were about to experience living here. So much room to run. Acres of wooded land to explore. So much to do. They would never be bored.

January came, and along with it came the cold weather, which added workloads of keeping the coal and wood stove burning. I was still unpacking boxes from our move. The third move in one year. That was a lot to deal with. And on top of all that I found out I was pregnant with baby number six! After leaving the Amish we did practice birth control, but that did not stop fertile Myrtle me from getting pregnant. I didn't know how we were going to make it with six babies, but I knew God would make a way.

The one thing I will be forever grateful to Mark for is the fact I could stay home and raise my children. He worked very hard to provide for his ever-growing family. To me that meant the world. I wanted to be the one to raise my sons. No one could love and care for them like their own mother. Proverbs 22:6 says, "Train up a child in the way that he should go, and when he is old, he will not depart from it." I wanted to raise my children according to scripture.

Even though our home was a dysfunctional one, I had a deep yearning in my heart to create a healthy, happy environment for my sons. They, like all normal children, needed this in order to grow up as healthy adults. The positive reports from the teachers told me they were doing well. Sebastian loved life, and when he missed a day of school his teacher said it was like the sun didn't shine that day. He was a ray of sunshine in my life as well. He was my willing helper. Even at his young age he felt a sense of responsibility for his brothers and in helping me too.

I was pleasantly surprised at how well the boys adapted back into their normal routine at school and how things seemed to fall into place. Caleb loved his friends, both Amish and non-Amish. His heart did not differentiate between the two. The one thing none of us liked was the hour-long bus ride to and from school. They dreaded it each morning. Wyatt, Alex and Nathan busied themselves with the toy box or chasing each other throughout the house while the two older boys were in school. They entertained each other well. I was thankful for that.

It took more time than I could find to do laundry, cleaning, cooking, and dishes. It seemed as soon as one meal was over, I was starting on the next one. It was a never-ending job to keep five hungry, rambunctious boys fed from early morning to evening bedtime. But I loved it. Right then, in that moment, there was nothing I'd rather do than to raise my gang of boys along with their squabbles, bumps, bruises and all that went along with raising these little guys.

There were those timeout moments with nowhere to hide when I had to take a few minutes, even if it meant locking myself in the bathroom, just to take a deep breath and hear myself think. During this time, I missed my mom and my sisters in such a painful way. If only I could talk to them, lean on them, have their love and support. I realize in their minds I was the one being uncooperative or rebellious. How I wish I could make them see that this is not the case. Far from it!

If I ever had a closer walk with Christ, it was during these times. When pain gets too overwhelming to bear alone, there is nowhere to go but to Christ. I remember so well in those excruciating times when I poured my heart out to my friend Sharon. She would say, "Eirene, when you get to the bottom, there is nowhere to go but up. Look up to your heavenly Father." And so I did. I cried and prayed and prayed some more. I would pray God's Word back to Him. I would remind Him that He would not give me more than I could bear. There were times when I wondered if He had overestimated my tolerance. I knew His Word was true. I kept telling myself this too shall pass; countless times I would repeat that phrase. I would also pray according to Philippians 4:13. I can do all things through Christ which strengthens me. This gave me much-needed comfort and strength. I also reminded myself many times that all I needed to be concerned about is today. There were those moments when I literally had to take life minute by minute. To think hours or days ahead was just too overwhelming.

Chapter 6

Having the support of my new church family gave me strength and a sense of belonging, something that we left behind when we left the Amish community. That is one of the many things I've always admired about my people, the Amish—that community support. I love the way they come together, helping those in need. I've seen a barn raised in a day, men and boys lending a helping hand. Very hard-working people, both men and women, young and old. The women would cook lots of food for the hard-working crews. It is still like that to this day. I loved the quiltings, where the women would gather together and make quilts, and the fellowship that went along with it. Precious memories never to be forgotten.

I continued to make many new friends in the church I now attended. My husband, Mark, was not as excited about going to church or meeting new people as I was, but there were a few of them that he accepted and eventually became good friends with. One couple in particular was John and Toni VanGordon. They were the kind of genuine, down-to-earth people that you just wanted to be with. John even started working with Mark when he needed an extra hand. They had two children, a daughter and a son. Having friends like them gave me hope that maybe Mark would eventually decide he wanted to stop the alcohol addiction and live a Christian life. Just maybe the influence of strong, loving Christians would help him want that life for us and our boys. I fasted and prayed and pleaded with God to let it be so.

We got to be really good friends, which was a good thing because one night in February when they came to visit, it snowed so much that it wasn't safe for them to leave and venture out on the road. Mark and John decided the best thing for them to do was spend the night. It continued to snow with blizzardlike conditions, and so John, Toni and the kids stayed for four days. What an adventure that was!

Mark, John and all the boys loved going outside and playing in the snow. The boys did a lot of sledding, and making snowmen was fun too. Trying to keep everyone fed for four days was a huge challenge. I think we were all on the verge of tears by the time the fourth day came and they could go home safely. Of course, me being pregnant with baby number six just made this experience more difficult.

February turned into March and then April. Sweet springtime, my very favorite time of year when the tree buds started to pop and Easter lilies would bloom, bringing with it bright colors, and everything came to life again. The time of year when I looked forward to planting my garden and landscaping and mowing the lawn. These were some of the activities that I loved to do. It felt therapeutic.

I loved the warm sunshiny days when the boys and I could be outside most of the day. For the most part they played well together. The younger boys entertained each other by playing in the sandbox while the older ones went to school. They were always happy to see them hop off the bus in the afternoon. There were also the days when all the boys got creative and pulled our big trampoline up close to the barn. Then they would climb up to the loft and open the window and jump out onto the trampoline! Wow! What one didn't think of, the others did. There was never a dull moment!

It was a beautiful day in July. I had been working in the yard all day, weeding the garden and mowing the lawn. All five of my little boys were outside with me. Wyatt and Alex were playing in the sandbox, and little two-year-old Nathan was toddling alongside them. Sebastian and Caleb were in the barn hammering away, building something or other. Those two little guys were creative and never ran out of something to do. I totally enjoyed my days outside with them.

I decided to cook dinner on the grill because it was such a beautiful day. As I was grilling the meat, I played my favorite music on my cassette player. Life seemed peaceful. About this time Mark came home from work. As he walked toward the house, taking in the activities and the freshly mowed grass, he looked at me and said something I will never forget. He said, "If you would do this every day, I would not have to drink!" What? I didn't say anything as I carried the grilled meat into the house, but that statement burned into my brain. I was confused. Just didn't make sense to me. According to his words I was responsible for his addictions! Just didn't seem fair to pile that burden on a wife's shoulders!

I was in the third trimester of my pregnancy. This little one was kicking into my ribs and was a very active baby. I counted the weeks and days to the due date. Being pregnant in the hot summer was not easy. But I was so thankful that now we had an air conditioner, which helped me have some much-needed rest. I wondered every day if this one would finally be my long-awaited daughter. I would just have to wait and see since we were not going to do an ultrasound to find out the gender of the baby.

This was the first pregnancy that I experienced alone, without my sisters and my mom. This was actually a year of many firsts. First year without my extended family. First year of surviving without their help, love or support. And again, I was extremely thankful for my dear friend Sharon. She was there for me, helping me out as much as possible. She truly was a lifesaver for me. I do want and need to give credit to my baby sister Margaret. She did come to my house to check in with me occasionally. She is very near and dear to my heart. If there is such a thing as a perfect sister, it is her. She is one in a million and loved by everyone. I am eternally grateful for her.

Each one of the boys had their own unique personality, which kept things interesting. Sebastian, the responsible one, felt responsible for the whole family at a very young age and always tried to keep everyone safe. Caleb was a helpful young man, very soft-hearted with a determination out of this world. I had never seen a young boy with such ambition and determination.

Then came quiet Wyatt, who was very bashful and stayed out of everyone's way for the most part. He is a middle child, and oftentimes when I hadn't seen or heard him, I'd go looking for him. Invariably I'd find him curled up in a chair asleep or sitting outside by an anthill, watching the ants making their homes. He would sit for hours watching them. He was a very deep thinker.

Then there was Alex, my ornery, energetic and rambunctious kid who was fearless. Alex was the kid who would give me my gray hairs and try my patience. Number five was Nathan, who loved following his brothers all over the place, out to the barn and into the woods, where they built their own little tree house. They never ran out of ideas.

And then there was Luke, my sweet little Luke, who would forever be my little boy. Since I'd had a tubal ligation after he was born, I knew he was going to be my last baby, and I wanted to enjoy each and every minute of the baby stage. I might have spoiled him a bit too much, but it didn't seem to hurt him. He was a happy-go-lucky little guy. He loved life and was always hungry. He must've been the hungriest little guy I'd ever seen. I was forever cooking in the kitchen to fill six little bellies. I loved every minute, no matter how tired I was. I enjoyed raising my children. I poured my heart and soul into them. They were my reason to live.

As a young girl, I looked up to Loretta Lynn. I always thought she was living my dream. I wanted to be just like her. After all, her childhood was very similar to mine. She grew up in the hollers of Kentucky with the poor people, running around barefoot all summer long. Her dad would buy new shoes once a year for her when winter would set in. Loretta got married at a very young age, and so did I. It was actually her husband who discovered Loretta's talent and pushed her to fame. She had a talent that she didn't even realize she had.

I admired Loretta and "Doolittle" (her husband) for their perseverance and hard work, which made them famous. So while Loretta was on stage singing, I was happy to stay home and raise my children. I could not bear the thought of leaving them for a babysitter or someone else to raise. They were my life, my responsibility. I wanted to be the one to read them Bible stories before they went to bed and make sure they were taken care of. I loved being their mother. I didn't have material things to spoil them with, but they never went to bed hungry; I made sure of that. I feel like I spoiled them with my good cooking, which they still enjoy to this day.

On many occasions it felt scary to me to raise my children outside of the Amish community. It was excruciatingly painful not to be able to share my boys with my parents, and the reality that my boys could not be with their grandparents, uncles, aunts and cousins was just too much. My boys had many questions which I could not answer, and it was hurtful for them. They just couldn't understand the reason. There were many, many, many times when I wondered if I was doing right by them. But at the same time, I knew I had to follow Christ. I read in the book of Matthew where it reads "He that loveth father or mother more than me is not worthy of me: and he that loveth son or daughter more than me is not worthy of me." So no matter what it cost—even if it cost my life— I was going to serve my God.

I was also determined to teach my boys how to serve God. I wanted them to know Him on a personal level. I wanted so much more for them than I had ever experienced. No matter how much it hurt me, I was willing to do it for them. The one thing that I wanted to give them more than anything else was a healthy home life—a safe environment and a healthy relationship with their daddy. But that was the very thing I could not give to them.

Our home was very dysfunctional. The alcohol addiction was rampant not only in our home but also in both my husband's and my own family upbringing. It is a very destructive addiction that affects each family member in a negative and painful way. Alcohol addiction or any addiction that controls the home environment is not conducive to a healthy upbringing for children.

I cried out to God many, many times. I asked Him to be the heavenly Father to my boys that their earthly father could not or would not be to them. He was my only hope, and I knew that He would be true to His Word. I found my peace, comfort and strength reading the Word of God.

Chapter 7

After I left the Amish community, which included all my family and friends, my social life suffered a bit, so I was ever so grateful for Sundays when I could go to church and be a part of like-minded believers. However, it was difficult trying to take five kids to church by myself. I felt that was where they needed to be, in church. In the presence of God. They couldn't understand why they had to sit in church if their daddy didn't go. This of course created confusion in their young minds. So many changes in a short time. How I wished it could have been different. How much better it would have been if my husband and I could have connected spiritually and worshipped in church together as a Christian couple should. It would have made the transition into a whole new world so much easier. It would also have been a great example to my boys of how a Christian couple should live.

Summer turned to fall, and along with that came—guess what—another boy! Baby boy number six. Luke was the smallest baby out of all six boys, weighing eight pounds. Dark hair and eyes. What a beautiful baby. This was another first. First time giving birth to a baby outside of the Amish community.

Mark had come to the hospital to be with me. At this particular hospital they served a steak dinner to the parents of a newborn. We had a pleasant dinner for two, which was a rare occasion. We had hired a babysitter to stay with the boys. So it was nice! Mark drove himself to the hospital; therefore he was sober. It was just the two of us alone with baby Luke. It was a nice, rare and special experience. Moments like this always sparked hope for a better, healthier future for us and our beautiful family.

27

I was anxious to get home to my little guys. How I missed them. This was the first time I had to leave them overnight since we left our Amish community, and it was probably harder on me than them.

It was chaotic to say the least after the sixth baby was born and Mark went back to work. The two oldest boys were in school. It left me with four little guys. Wyatt was at the age where I could have started him in kindergarten, but I did not see my way clear to take him and pick him up from school with three babies. So we waited until the following year, thinking we could start him and Alex at the same time since they were only sixteen months apart, but the school wouldn't have it that way, and so it was decided Wyatt would go into first grade and Alex into kindergarten.

Wyatt was academically advanced, and so it was easy for him to go into first grade. Besides that, he had the absolute best teacher in the world, Mrs. Sorg, who was so sweet, loving, kind and patient, which is exactly what Wyatt needed. He was the absolute most quiet son I have ever had. He was a very deep thinker, but he knew how to take care of himself. He had to since he was still a baby, not even walking by himself when I gave birth to Alex. He actually decided to walk that first week after Alex was born. It was almost like having twins, considering the mountains of laundry I washed each day, in addition to trying to keep everyone fed and the dishes done. Not to mention gardening and canning fruits, vegetables, soups and salsa.

It was a cool October day. Sebastian and Caleb had gotten on the bus. Wyatt, Alex and Nathan were in the living room watching cartoons and I was sitting in my rocking chair, feeding baby Luke and reflecting on the changes over the past few weeks. What a life-changing experience a new baby brings into the world. I felt like our family was now complete. I knew I wasn't going to give birth to any more babies and I wanted to enjoy every moment of this newborn phase. Luke was a sweet baby. Content as long as he was fed and had a clean diaper. He was so adorable. His dark hair was sweaty as he ate hungrily. Not a worry in the world. He slept well at night, which was a great help for this busy mama. I needed all the rest I could possibly get.

As I sat in the rocker feeding Luke, I thought about how different it was this time. None of the usual family visits like we had after all the other babies. I really missed not having my mom or sisters come to visit. I felt hurt and abandoned, but I understood why they couldn't come to my house, since we had left the church. Somehow it seemed like such unnecessary pain. I was serving God the best I knew how but was being shunned because I served Him in a way they didn't agree with. I often wondered how God saw all this division in the name of religion. All I wanted was to serve Him. As I rocked little Luke, I rested his head against my shoulder. As he slept, I talked to my heavenly Father and read scripture. This is where I found peace and courage to go on—these times when I could lay my burdens at His feet according to 1 Peter 5:7. "Casting all your care upon him; for he careth for you." Such love. Such peace. If only I could share this with my husband. I wanted so much to experience this Christian walk with him.

Looking at the clock, I knew it was time to put little Luke to bed and get some laundry done. The boys were getting restless and bored with cartoons, so they went outside to play. I was thankful they entertained each other so well.

As I tackled my chores, the workload suddenly seemed like an impossible task. Especially with a newborn baby. So much to do and not enough time in the day to get everything done besides the obvious: cooking, dishes, laundry and cleaning. How was I ever going to get it all done?

There was also the garden. Weeds needed to be pulled. Canning had to be done. Every year I would can several hundred quarts of different kinds of soups, such as chili, vegetable and tomato soup. I would also can fruits and vegetables and salsa—lots of salsa. The boys loved it. It was necessary to get all the canning done to get us through the winter months when Mark's construction work dwindled down and finances became even tighter.

As I allowed the overwhelming feelings to overtake me, I went into the bathroom because I didn't want my boys to see their mommy cry. With tears streaming down my face, sobbing, I allowed myself to just feel all the feelings of helplessness and the pain of being completely alone. I had never needed the love, help and support of my family as I did at this moment. I needed my mom. I needed my sisters. I just needed help and the feeling of family support. These tasks loomed so large and seemed so impossible. It would not have seemed like such an impossible task if I could've counted on Mark to come home and give me a hand after work, but I did not have his comfort or support. His addiction got first dibs before me, my chores or our children. All I could do was rely on my Savior to see me through. I just had to trust Him. This definitely required a lot of faith muscle. I reminded myself that God would never give me more than I could bear. At a time like this I reminded Him of that.

While Luke slept, I went out to the garden and left the dishes for later. This would give me at least two hours to pull weeds and gather some vegetables. I could get a lot done as long as the rest of the boys played in the sandbox. I was ever so thankful that they could entertain each other so well.

As I worked in the garden and listened to the chitter-chatter of the boys in the sandbox, my mind fast-forwarded to the months ahead. I was thinking about the holidays and wondered how we would be able to get through them without our extended families this first year of leaving the community. I was thinking maybe we could have Thanksgiving dinner with some of our new friends, like the VanGordons. I knew somehow we would get through the Thanksgiving holiday, but I just couldn't imagine Christmas without my parents.

This holiday was always a big deal. We would all get together at my parents' house along with my brothers and sisters and their families. This year they would have it without us. Once again that was a painful thought. All I could do was live moment by moment, literally. I couldn't allow myself to think about tomorrow or next week or next month and all of the what-ifs that go along with it.

"Mom, I'm hungry!" The boys called out to me as they came to the garden. "What can we eat?" A very familiar question. I gathered up all the green beans I had harvested and put all the weeds on a pile for the older boys to get rid of when they got home from school and followed my little guys into the house, where we got cleaned up and I prepared a quick lunch of vegetable soup and peanut butter and jelly sandwiches. They devoured the food like hungry little bears.

I quickly diapered and fed little Luke. Sweet little Luke. Not a care in the world. Such an adorable little bundle. I loved his sweet baby smells and our bonding time as I laid him up against my shoulder so he could burp after his feeding. I wished I had more time to just hold and enjoy him, but the laundry needed to be done or we wouldn't have clean clothes to wear. So I put Luke in his baby seat and tackled the job at hand.

Here came the bus. Oh my! Where had the day gone? I was always happy to see my two oldest boys come home from school and so were their little brothers. They usually had a lot to say about the day's happenings in school as they devoured their snacks. Sebastian talked highly of his teacher, whom he adored. They seemed to have a very good relationship, which was a good thing because Sebastian struggled academically. He did not enjoy learning in school. Many times he would beg to stay home.

Caleb seemed to enjoy his friends more than his studies. He got along well with his classmates. Overall they both seemed to be adjusting very well in school. I had feared the worst, so it was a relief to see them adjust well so quickly.

After having snacks and conversations as I fed baby Luke yet again, the four older boys took little two-year-old Nathan outside, where they played in the sandbox and did what little boys do. It was amazing how long they could stay busy in the sandbox with water trickling from the hose. They created farms and ditches. To me it looked like a muddy mess, but to the boys it was a big farm. How they loved it.

I tried to hurry and finish the laundry while planning what to have for dinner. In a few hours Mark would be home from work, and I wanted to make sure the boys were fed before he got home. In our dysfunctional home it was much better to be done with feeding six boys rather than trying to eat together as a family. Things were way too tense. Along with Mark's alcohol addiction, he also suffered from a bipolar disorder, which made things really difficult. It was like walking on eggshells. Most of the time this was the absolute most dreaded time of the day. The smallest little thing could set him off. This kind of dysfunction affected the whole family.

I often hurt for the little ones who did not understand why life was so painful and confusing. I wanted so much for healing to take place, not only for his sake but for the boys as well. They needed a healthy, godly example of a father and it was not happening. I did the one thing I could do and that was PRAY! I had to trust and believe that God would heal, lead and guide my boys through life. It was the only way I could function. I lived one day at a time. And sometimes I literally lived hour by hour. It was too overwhelming to think days and weeks ahead. I had to remind myself that this too shall pass.

Sometimes when things would get too overwhelming, I would go pick up my Bible and just open it. Many, many times it landed on a perfect word. Exactly what I needed at that moment. God is so good like that. The scripture in Philippians 4:19 says, "But my God shall supply all your need according to his riches in glory by Christ Jesus." And it is true. He has always provided just the right word at the time of need. I was so thankful to have a close relationship with my God. Unbearable situations became bearable with His help. Truly I can do all things through Christ which strengthens me (Philippians 4:13).

So many painful changes because of the decision to leave all to obey and follow Christ. I knew that God would not ask me to go through anything that He hadn't already gone through first. And I knew without a doubt that with His help, nothing would be too hard to endure.

Chapter 8

After moving into our forever home, we started to add things like TVs, stereos, and other tech toys. Neither Mark nor I were tech-savvy. We had just bought our first stereo from a garage sale. We worked and worked on it. We couldn't get it to play. We pushed buttons, turned knobs, plugged and unplugged it. Nothing worked! Sebastian kept insisting he could make it work. He just knew he could do it. Finally, after fiddling with it for a long time, Mark and I gave up and walked away, leaving it to the kids to play with. Lo and behold, it wasn't even five minutes when Sebastian had music playing from the stereo. Beaming, he said, "See! I told you I can make it work." Of course, he was right. I was amazed! Sebastian was great at figuring things out on his own. He was a very brilliant and creative young man. He thought ahead and had many dreams. He would be my inventor. That was one of his many dreams.

I realized I was blessed beyond my dreams with six beautiful, awesome, ornery, cute, rambunctious boys. I loved them more than life. My greatest desire and goal was to see them saved, ensuring eternal salvation in heaven. Everything else was secondary. Oh, how I loved these precious little boys. They were my life. My reason for living. I wanted to give them so much more than I was able to. What I couldn't provide for them in material things I made up for by doing things for them, such as cooking their favorite meals, etc. I loved them through praying and providing for them spiritually. Many times I denied my own needs in order to be able to give to them.

My thoughts often took me to a what-if dreamland. What if I would've been able to choose my career or make my own choices and decisions in life? What if I would have been privileged enough to choose whether or not I would have an education? How far would I have gone? Who would I be today? A doctor? A nurse? A nurse practitioner? An alternative health practitioner? I will never have the answers to these questions, but one thing I could do was become a reflexologist, which is exactly what I did. I loved to learn, and one of the subjects I was interested in was the human body.

That is why I contacted Jennifer Gaerke (now Cheeseman), who practiced alternative health such as reflexology and iridology. She helped me to get to the right classes that taught the Ingham Method of Reflexology. I absolutely loved it and absorbed the information like a sponge.

Jennifer allowed me to come into her practice, where I had hands-on learning. She told me that I was a natural at it. I was very impressed with Jennifer's expertise. She was an amazing instructor. To this day my family and I are forever grateful for her guidance and leadership. Whenever my boys had sore muscles, headaches or just didn't feel good, they would always ask Mom for a foot treatment, which helped them feel better. And so, for many, many years I would treat feet. Hundreds of people would find my foot treatments relaxing. Treating people's feet gave me a sense of purpose and fulfillment, and some made small financial donations, which I was ever so grateful for.

My boys were growing up very quickly, and little Luke was sixteen months old already. He wasn't feeling well one day. I did the normal vitamin drops and Vicks on his chest, but he just wasn't getting any better. Mark had gone to work as usual and the older boys went to school. It was me and the four little boys at home. Luke was running a temperature, and his breathing was labored. I called a friend, who agreed to come stay with the boys so I could take Luke in to the doctor's office. She agreed to stay until I came home or until Mark would get home from work. Here again was a very painful time of needing my mother or brothers or sisters and not being able to reach out to them.

Dr. Judge looked at baby Luke. After checking his oxygen level, temperature and everything else, he said, "Take this baby straight to the hospital. I'll call ahead so they'll be ready for you."

My heart hurt for my little Luke, who was so sick. He was pale and listless. His chest heaved heavily with every breath he took. I prayed all the way to the hospital. As soon as we got there, the doctor and nurses took over. They immediately placed him in the oxygen tent and started meds intravenously. Luke did not appreciate the oxygen tent. He cried and screamed and fought them. His oxygen level was dangerously low. There was no other way to provide him with oxygen but to keep him in the tent, and so the medical team asked me to get into the tent with him! And so I did! Fortunately for me I was pretty tiny back then, which made it possible to be in the tent with baby Luke.

The doctor made it very clear we were not going home that day. I just didn't know what to do or which way to turn. Who would feed my boys and tuck them into bed? How would I get a change of clothes? I just wanted to cry. I called Mark, and he agreed to take care of the boys and feed them and put them to bed. The babysitter agreed to stay again the next day.

Mark brought me some clothes. He couldn't stand being inside a hospital, so he didn't waste any time leaving as soon as possible. I stayed by Luke's side, never leaving to make phone calls or take a shower or anything unless he was fast asleep, and then I had to rush to be back by his side before he'd wake up and panic.

I was very anxious. Watching for any sign of improvement. Anything that would give me hope or encouragement that my baby was healing and that we could go home to family, but it didn't happen. His breathing seemed very labored. He looked at me as if to beg Mommy to make him better. It hurt to watch him struggle. The doctor made his rounds and said he'd be back in a few hours.

As I held Luke in my arms, his breathing seemed to be getting worse, not better. Hour after hour dragged by with no improvements. Finally, another doctor on call came to check in on Luke and saw that his condition was worsening and said we might have to transfer him to a bigger hospital! My heart sank. This surely was just a bad dream. This could not be happening to my little Luke. Another doctor was called in for a second opinion, and he also agreed that they needed to get him to another hospital as soon as possible. I was in panic mode as I once again called Mark to tell him what was happening.

Everything seemed to go into slow motion after that. The ambulance pulled up and the doctors and nurses feverishly worked on Luke, taking him out of the oxygen tent and securing a portable oxygen mask to his face. They would not even transport him from his hospital bed to the ambulance without oxygen.

This was looking really, really bad, and silently I was crying out to God; He was all I had. I did not have my husband by my side. I did not have my mom or my sisters or any family member or friend to do this with me. I felt completely helpless and alone. I was very scared as I listened to the emergency technician call ahead to the hospital where we were being transported to with lights and sirens blaring. They described him as a 16-month-old male, semi-conscious, labored breathing. I remember thinking I might lose my baby.

As soon as we arrived at Lutheran Hospital in Fort Wayne, there was a team of doctors and nurses lined up on both sides of the emergency room, waiting to whisk my baby away the minute we got there. I followed them as they rushed him into a room, laid him on the table and feverishly worked on him. They attached him to machines and hoses, and poked him with needles. I felt so helpless as he cried in pain with every needle poke. He looked back at me as if to beg me to protect him from the pain and suffering. I knew I had to stay strong for him, but I was about to lose it. If only I had someone, anyone, to go through this with me, but I had no one. Me and God. That's it! I had to live by faith, minute by excruciating minute.

I finally decided to call a friend to go tell my family what was happening. I thought surely in a desperate situation like this they would be able to look past our differences and come and be with me in the hospital for at least an hour or two. They did call me and said if we were still in the hospital by Thursday they would come and visit. Luke had been in the hospital for two days already. We all thought for sure he'd get to go home soon. Wednesday brought some improvements, but the doctor decided Luke needed to stay in the hospital for a while longer. Thursday came, and I still had no visitors!

The days dragged by. No visitors. No one. No family. No friends. Not even Mark since the rest of the boys needed him at home. Since I had been promised by my Amish family that they would come visit if we hadn't gone home yet, my hopes were high that I would get to see them. So I walked the halls. Back and forth. Back and forth for hours on end, watching and waiting. Hoping against hope to catch a glimpse of my mom, my sisters, someone, anyone. The doctors allowed me to put Luke in a little stroller and push him up and down the hall. He had made a huge improvement and was happy to get out of that hospital crib. Nighttime came and my heart sank as I finally accepted the fact that no one was coming to visit. What a brutal, excruciating week with no visitors. This is the price I pay to follow Jesus. I accepted that fact.

Finally, Friday morning the doctors released little Luke from the hospital, and I was excited to go home to my dear boys. They missed me as much as I missed them. But we were all happy to be home. All together in one place. Looking around, I saw all the work waiting for me! It was quite obvious I hadn't been home all week, but I didn't mind. I had all six of my boys around me once again.

Chapter 9

Mark's Aunt Katy would periodically send us cards and messages for us to stop by and see her. Even though she was a devout member of the Amish church, she made exceptions and tried to stay in contact with us without getting in trouble with the preachers. I was grateful for her. She was a small lady, never got married, and made a living by taking care of the elderly. She would live with people she was caring for, and that is how she died. Taking care of others. She reminded me of Mother Theresa. It was a sad time when she passed away.

Mark and I decided to get a sitter for the boys and attend Katy's funeral. We knew it would be a very awkward time since we were being shunned. Mark's dad told us to sit with the family by Aunt Katy's casket, which was pretty close to where the preachers were sitting. I was wondering if they would allow us to stay there. I didn't have long to think about it. I overheard Bishop Henry tell the rest of the preachers he had a problem with Mark and me being in the same room as the family. After discussing it for a few minutes, they decided to tell us to leave the room. They pointed to a small, empty back room, where Mark and I sat through the remainder of the funeral. This gave us an idea of how Jesus must have felt many times when the Pharisees ridiculed and shunned Him. The pain of rejection! I still don't understand how they think pushing us away would draw us back to them. This was the opposite of God's love. It just didn't make sense to me.

The years sped by. The boys were now at an age where they became interested in sports at school. Sebastian took an interest in wrestling while Caleb loved football. Having been raised Amish, I hadn't the first clue about any sport or how to help my boys be part of those programs. I stumbled through it the best I could by talking to the parents of friends the boys made at school. I tried to share their excitement, but inside I was very apprehensive about contact sports and whether the boys should or should not participate.

If only I didn't have to make all these decisions alone. Aren't these two-parent decisions? How to cope! It became increasingly difficult to make these decisions alone. As I watched the boys at their practice sessions, there were a few moms but mostly dads coaching their sons or cheering them on. How I wished my boys would have that kind of relationship with their dad.

I will never ever forget Caleb's first football game. I was sitting in the bleachers with five boys while their brother Caleb played his first game. I didn't know the first thing about football, so when the crowd went crazy watching Caleb run the ball across the length of the field and make a touchdown, I realized he must've done something great. They were on their feet, screaming Caleb's name. Looking around, I heard them ask the question, "Where are this kid's parents?" Of course, I was too bashful to let them know it was me.

My heart felt like it was about to burst with pride and excitement for my son, and I so much wanted to stand up and wave my arms and say, "Me! I am his mother! Caleb is my son!" How I wished I could have shared this moment with my husband, who didn't have enough interest to be there with us. I had never been to a football game in my life. This was a new and exciting experience for the boys and myself. I was loving this new phase in our new world.

One by one the boys found their own niche in sports. Sebastian was content wrestling. His strength and interests were more in the brilliance of his mind. He talked a lot about inventions and becoming an inventor. I loved his enthusiasm and creativity. Caleb loved football and weightlifting. At 12 years old he was carrying two five-gallon buckets of water, one in each hand. He lifted them simultaneously as high as he could. He had persistence and determination that amazed me.

Wyatt and Alex would soon follow in the footsteps of their older brothers in the sports realm. This kept me a very busy mama driving back and forth from school to home and back to school again, making multiple trips a day. But I loved it. I absolutely put my heart and soul into the lives of my boys. Enjoying these first-time, new activities with them and learning as we went was a positive experience for me and my boys.

There were many times I wished their father would take an interest and be an example to his sons, bond with them and coach them. My sons will never have that experience. Fortunately they had great coaches who took an interest in them and grew to know them individually. They each had their favorite coach. I was thankful for that.

Each time my boys experienced a victory it was a proud mama moment—one I so desperately wanted to share with someone such as their dad, grandparents, aunts, uncles and cousins, but we were alone in that world of sports. We did have the families of their teammates, which helped some.

It was pretty tough keeping up with the diets and regimens required to keep their goal weights in wrestling. At times they needed to lose two pounds or wrestle in a higher weight class, which meant they needed the right kinds of food and rest and exercise. I remember them having to run and run and run to make the weight class and packing their breakfast so as not to eat a meal until after weigh-in. I was so grateful to be a part of moments like this.

It was July 11th, a beautiful, sunshiny day. Going to a funeral was the last thing I wanted to do, but at the same time I wanted to show support for my friend Betty, whose dad had passed away. I'd never met him personally, but I knew he was a great guy by the number of people who showed up at the funeral. And he was dearly loved by his family.

As I was sitting with my friends, observing people—something I like to do—I saw a strikingly beautiful lady walk in. She was dark complected, her black hair was long and curly, she had beautiful dark eyes, and she wore a light blue dress. It was all I could do to stop myself from going to greet her. There was something very special about her, and there was an unexplainable familiarity about her. I just had to meet her. I thought maybe I'd say hi after the funeral was over, but my bashful self couldn't muster up the courage, and so after everything was over, I said my goodbyes to Betty and her family. Giving them my condolences, I left and decided to stop at Walmart.

I did my shopping, and as I went through the checkout I saw her again— the beautiful lady from the funeral. She was also going through the checkout, same time as me. I thought, *I'm not leaving until I say hi to this girl.* I felt like I just had to know who she was and where she came from. So I walked outside the building and waited for her to come out. I didn't have long to wait. In a few short minutes, here she came.

 Lo and behold, she walked right up to me and said, "Hi, I'm Carmen. You look so familiar!" We shook hands and talked for quite some time. We discovered that our paths had crossed indirectly. We both knew a lot of the same people. We both had gone to the funeral in support of the family. Neither one of us knew the deceased. I was ecstatic to have met my forever best friend that day. We exchanged phone numbers and have never lost touch.

I believe with all my heart that God knew that Carmen and I needed each other for friendship and support. We had so much in common, including our dysfunctional homes with absentee fathers. We both experienced the wrath of living with alcoholism and addictions. We both were very familiar with unstable home environments. We both wanted so much more for our children. She had two girls who were twins! And a son. She had three children; I had six! It seemed supernatural how she always knew when I was going through a struggle and vice versa.

When I was having a bad day, she would call and check on me. Somehow she knew. I didn't have to say a word. Just knowing she was in my world was very comforting. I'll be forever grateful to my Lord for her. True friends are priceless. Worth more than gold.

Carmen was the kind of friend everyone wants. I knew I could trust her with my deepest secrets. We had that for each other. No matter what, we had each other's backs. She was very much loved by everyone who knew her, including my boys. When she called, my boys liked to answer the phone just to tease her. They loved the back and forth bantering she was so good at. She could put a smile on anyone's face. She had that happy, bubbly personality that was so contagious. She truly was a godsend to me.

Forsaking all for the sake of Christ is not an easy life to live, especially when there is opposition in the home. The book of Matthew talks about how a house divided against itself cannot stand. Along with a divided home comes a lot of stress, which was what I was living—a very stressful life. It began to take its toll on me physically. I began to experience panic attacks and severe debilitating migraines to the point where I couldn't get out of bed for days. The really painful, nauseating kind that caused vomiting and blurry vision. My left arm and leg started to feel numb. I would not wish this sickness on anyone. It was very miserable. No pain medication seemed to give me any relief.

Mark had his hands full during these terrible, trying times. Thankfully I had friends and neighbors willing to lend a hand, as well as a very faithful babysitter. Her name was Rachel. She was a trustworthy and competent young lady who was brave enough to take on six boys and babysit them. I was very, very thankful for Rachel. She was my lifeline and gave me much-needed breaks. It was during this time that someone referred me to a chiropractor in Fort Wayne, Indiana. I called them and set an appointment to see Dr. Alter. At that time there were two brothers working together in one office. They did an evaluation on me, and I was told that I had a pinched nerve in my neck, which was causing the numbness in my left arm and leg. I was hopeful that they could help me with my pinched nerve without surgery. They were willing to try!

And so I would drive to Fort Wayne, Indiana, three times a week, which was an hour drive one way and became very expensive with having to pay for gas and a babysitter and the chiropractor treatments. But I was willing to scrimp and save and cut corners in order to be healed without surgery. This went on for quite some time. The numbness started to improve, but the migraines were still severe.

I will never forget the day I went into Alter Chiropractic's office with a headache that made me feel exceptionally sick. I felt like I just couldn't move another step. I was nauseous and felt like I was going to vomit any minute. Dr. Alter came in to administer the adjustment, and a very young looking guy came in with him. Dr. Alter said, "This is my younger brother, Michael. He just graduated from chiropractic school. He will be joining us, if you don't mind." I literally felt sorry for the young man for having to help nauseous, sick people such as myself. He didn't seem to mind, however. And as time went on, he became my regular doctor that I went to see for adjustments.

I remember well the day I asked him if he thought he could ever get rid of my migraine headaches. His response was, "Give me a couple years." His confidence gave me hope and was very encouraging. Lo and behold, that is exactly what happened. My headaches became less severe and less frequent. I went from having a migraine every two weeks to every two months. Finally they completely disappeared. I believe God healed my headaches through Dr. Michael Alter, who is a very effective, successful chiropractor to this very day. He's helped countless people including many of my friends and family.

Chapter 10

As the years passed there were many changes. The boys were growing up quickly. Now they were all in school except for the youngest, little Luke. Along with growing boys came the need for a bigger house. We had often discussed the possibility of adding a bedroom and updating the kitchen and installing new cabinets. It was possible to do since Mark had his own construction crew and could do the work himself. He also had buddies that would come on the weekends and drink with him who were willing to help us with our huge project.

"Huge" might not be the correct adjective to describe the project we were about to begin. Instead of moving out of our home, we decided to do the remodeling while living in the house, which was a big mistake. It was overwhelming and extremely stressful. Mark and I both felt like we bit off more than we could chew. It took us a total of two months from start to finish and it was a big mess! We gutted the whole kitchen. We tore out walls. We added a whole new bedroom and bathroom. The boys hated the process. There was not a single clean spot to sit down for meals or anything. They were happy to leave the chaotic mess and go to school, where life seemed more normal.

The vision of the completed project is what helped me keep my sanity. Many times I'd take my little Luke and leave for the day. We would drop off the boys at school and go run errands or out to lunch. Luke liked to go to Pizza Hut. He enjoyed their salad bar, which seemed quite unusual for a little boy. On one of those days there was a table of police officers, and Luke went up to their table to say hi. It took me by surprise since he didn't normally initiate a conversation with strangers. Little did I know he would someday make this his profession. But for now he was content to hang out with his mother. I enjoyed him very much. I didn't like the thought of him going to school soon.

What would I ever do all day with all six boys in school? Go back to school myself perhaps! The thought of finishing my education and having my own career seemed very liberating and exciting. But for now I just wanted to enjoy raising my boys and getting my house back in order.

Things were starting to come together. The bedroom was framed. The drywall was being hung. Pretty soon I could start hanging wallpaper and do the painting, which I loved to do. Dan, a buddy of Mark's, helped build a wooden bar in our newly remodeled kitchen. It was absolutely beautiful and was made from trees that Dan had cut down himself, which made it even more special. It matched the wood floor and cabinets. What a beautiful home this was turning out to be.

The new bedroom suite had a cathedral ceiling, complete with a bathroom and closet! Wow! I began to feel like the queen of my castle after the project was completed. Completely finished. The windows in the kitchen and bedroom had been given new curtains, and carpet had been installed in the bedroom. It was more beautiful than I had dared to imagine. My newly remodeled home looked like a picture from a magazine! Such talent my husband had! I remember saying it was worth all the chaos we went through for two months. I couldn't wait to have friends over and show off my beautiful home. My feelings of gratitude were overwhelming. I never thought I'd ever have such a nice home.

Mark and I seemed to work together well on projects like remodeling. Often during the day he would ask me to meet him on his job and have lunch with him. We both enjoyed these moments. It seemed to me as long as he was sober and we didn't talk about church or the things of God we could tolerate each other. It was on weekends when he was drunk or out drinking with his buddies and I was in church or with Christian people that the tension and turmoil were the worst.

Many times when we were camping, I would take as many of the boys that would go with me to church, where we would be in a happy, peaceful atmosphere. Mark would stay at the campsite with the rest of our sons and cook on the grill and drink his beer. What a contrast to leave a spirit-filled church service and go back to a drunken, smoke-filled crowd where Mark and his buddies were drinking and every other word was a cuss word! How confusing this must've been to our young children. I couldn't do what I felt like doing, which was pack up and leave, so I stayed and tried to play the role of the good wife. We had some major differences, which caused both Mark and me to be frustrated and miserable. Oh, if only we could be team players.

Oftentimes I would observe married couples in church, worshipping together, loving each other. The husbands would be supportive in their role as spiritual leaders in the home. I could only try to imagine what that must feel like—a home with Christ as the foundation! How amazing that must be. Many times I wondered if these sisters realized how good they had it. Did they appreciate and respect their Christian husbands or take them for granted? I wondered if I would ever have the privilege of having that experience. The experience of sharing a Christian life with a like-minded husband who served the one true God and had a desire to see his children do the same. I tried to imagine what that would look like. Studying scripture together, singing songs together in worship, and praying together for us, our sons, and their future wives and families that were yet to come. Would Mark and I ever have that experience together? Only time would tell.

Chapter 11

God only knows all the trials and pains and sorrows that go along with raising six boys. Doctors' visits and hospital stays. These times would have been much more tolerable if we could've pulled together as a team. Like the time Wyatt had an appendicitis attack. Mark was away at work, out of state somewhere. I was alone with the six boys. Wyatt became very, very ill. I was on my own to find a babysitter so that I could take Wyatt to the doctor's office. He was pale and in severe pain. I had never seen him so sick before.

After checking him out and probing around on his stomach, which put Wyatt in unbearable pain, the doctor decided that he needed to go to the hospital for emergency surgery. Again, here I was! Alone to make these decisions and sit through hours of uncertainty. Wyatt was in misery and so scared. I tried to comfort him and pray for him. Why, I asked. Why was this happening? Why was I going through this alone? However, I was grateful that Wyatt at least had one parent with him, loving him and lifting him up in prayer.

After he was taken into surgery, I made phone calls to my friend Sharon, asking for prayers for Wyatt to get through this and heal quickly. It was getting really late. It seemed like an eternity since they had taken my little boy into surgery. What could be taking so long? Was Wyatt ok? How was he doing? If he woke up alone, he'd be afraid. All these thoughts and more kept going through my mind as I sat there hour after hour, waiting for him to be through surgery.

Finally! After what seemed like an eternity, the surgeon came into the consultation room to talk to me. He said Wyatt came in just in time. He said that he had gangrene in his appendix and if we would have waited longer, the appendix would have burst and Wyatt's health would have been in great danger. I called Mark to tell him the news. I could not hide my tears any longer. I asked him to hurry home as soon as possible. This was too much for a young mother to go through alone. How I wished I had someone by my side.

I did my best to comfort Wyatt. At the same time I felt like I needed comforting as well. I felt so alone. We never did these things alone in the Amish community. We supported each other. If one of us ended up in the hospital, we were surrounded by family. But now since I left the community, I was totally alone except for God. He truly was all I had. This drew me even closer to Him. He truly never leaves or forsakes us. I am so grateful.

After being in the hospital for a few days, Wyatt was released to go home. He was still pale but looking much better. He was happy to leave the hospital and get back to his brothers, who were very happy to see him. They joked with him to lighten his mood, but it hurt him to laugh. He was content to sit in the recliner, holding a pillow to his belly, and drink liquids and eat only light foods.

Just when Wyatt healed from his surgery and I thought life was getting back to normal, it happened again. This time it was Caleb. We were all outside one Sunday afternoon when all of a sudden Caleb doubled over in severe pain. It was relentless. No matter what he did, he found no relief. This time Mark was home. He picked Caleb up and put him over his shoulder and carried him to the car. Another emergency room visit with hours of waiting for a doctor to come in and perform more tests and lab work. How could this be happening again?

After all the testing and lab work, it was determined that we needed to talk to the surgeon, who confirmed that Caleb was having an appendicitis attack and needed to have his appendix removed. This time it was not as severe as it was with Wyatt. And this time Mark was there too. He wasn't about to spend the night inside the hospital, but at least he came with us and stayed until Caleb went through the surgery. This was so much better than doing it alone.

After a short hospital stay, Caleb was released to go home and recuperate. He was a strong young man, and it didn't take long for him to recover and be his normal, healthy self. I hoped and prayed we wouldn't have to go through this again. Two out of six boys with appendicitis was enough. I wondered if it could've been a hereditary weakness since their dad had his appendix removed when he was a third grader.

Hurry, hurry, hurry. Life just seemed so hectic and busy. With all six boys in school now, it seemed like I should be able to slow down just a little bit. It was time to reevaluate my life. I needed to think ahead. What did the future hold? I pondered and I prayed. I loved being a mom to my six boys more than anything in the world, but what about being a wife? Life kept me so busy that I didn't have time to think about my own emotions or needs. I hardly even knew who I was. *What do I want in life? What do I want to accomplish? Is this all there is to life? How can I make a difference in this world? What is my purpose on this earth?*

One thing I was very certain about was God did not intend for us to just exist. Didn't His Word teach us that He came so that we might have life and that more abundantly? Yes. That is what I wanted. A life full of abundance and purpose. Being able to make a difference! I wanted to reach out and help single moms. The struggle for these mothers is very real. But it wasn't just single moms who needed help. Some of them were just like me—legally married but feeling alone and single. Sometimes the pain of being married and alone is much more excruciatingly painful than being single and alone.

I experienced those times in our marriage when things became intolerable due to all the problems involved in a home of addiction and chaos and confusion. More times than I could count I yearned for us to be a Christian family serving God together, praying together, and doing life together instead of living a divided life. There were times when things got so intolerable that I would meet with my pastor and his wife. They were very familiar with our situation, and at times my pastor would encourage me to separate from my husband for a time. A break from each other might help us both to realize what was important in life.

These separations were extremely hard on all of us but especially hard on the boys. They felt insecure and unsettled. I regret some of those decisions to this day, but I had no perfect solutions. My options were very limited. I chose to be with my children if it killed me. Nothing would convince me that it was ok to put my own needs and desires before theirs. I gave birth to these little guys. They trusted me to care for them. I had a fierce mother's love and devotion for them. And for that reason I would not even consider following a career path until I finished raising them. I cut corners so that I could be able to stay home with them and keep them fed. In my mind there wasn't a babysitter in this world who could love them like I did.

During the day when all six of my boys were in school, I would think about all the what-ifs. What if I went back to school to finish my education? What is it that I would do? What kind of career would I enjoy? What career would financially provide the kind of life I would dream about? Where would I go? Could I financially support myself and my boys? Somehow just thinking about the possibilities gave me a glimmer of hope. I had read a lot of personal development books. Even though my Amish culture would not allow us to go to school past eighth grade, I never stopped learning. I had a hunger for knowledge, and somehow deep down inside of me I knew there was a better life ahead. I just knew it. The self-help books I read talked about how you bring about what you think about. I read in the Word of God that I can do all things through Christ which strengthens me (Philippians 4:13). I knew my God was more than able to do exceedingly above all I could think about.

It was about this time in my life when I was introduced to an amazing natural product called K-M, an herbal supplement distributed to the public through a networking system, where I would recruit people to become distributors of the product or retail customers. This would be my very first experience in a sales-based opportunity and would go hand in hand with my reflexology business. It would also be something I could do from home while working around my kids' schedules. I thought I would be able to help a lot of people both physically and financially.

So I became my own customer and tried the product. I liked the results, and my husband decided to try it as well. Lo and behold, after taking the K-M for a week or so he decided he didn't like it because it caused him to dislike the taste of beer. He decided to stay on it so that he could help me promote it as a business and soon we had recruited a group of people and I was excited about the possibilities. Most of the people I introduced the product to became customers or distributors. Within a short time, I had built an organization of 1000 people.

I began doing individual and group trainings and even became a speaker for my organization. This was a huge turning point in my life, and it seemed like our marriage began to heal. Mark and I finally had something in common—something we both liked. Our business skyrocketed to the point that we were going on company-sponsored trips and vacations. We were even featured in Matol's company magazine as top distributors.

Mark and I were given the opportunity to fly to Hawaii to a company-sponsored event with almost all of the expenses paid for. I was ecstatic, more so than Mark. He was afraid to fly. It was useless to try to convince him to go because his mind was made up. He said he would stay home with the four youngest boys if I would take the two oldest with me. Needless to say, it was an unforgettable experience.

It was the first time in my life that I was treated like royalty. I felt as if I was dreaming. The lights, glitz and glamor. The posh hotels and the limousines. The food! Oh my goodness! The food looked too pretty to eat. Food and drinks were everywhere. Beautiful music was playing. I had never seen anything like it. I was getting a taste of luxury and I liked it! It seemed heavenly. I imagined heaven must be something like this.

It was also an unforgettable experience for Sebastian and Caleb. They loved walking the streets, where they saw fishponds and beautiful nature. Each morning we would get up early and walk by the ocean in the soft white sand on the beach and enjoy the early morning salt air. We enjoyed the sounds of the waves and seagulls. We felt like all was well with the world. We marveled at how there were no bugs. We would always find a restaurant with outdoor seating and eat breakfast outdoors. We saw no flies or bugs. It was amazing. This was one of the highlights of my life. I discovered that I loved sales and the freedom it provided.

But it really was too good to be true. Approximately two years into the program, the company went bankrupt and brought my newfound freedom to a sudden halt. It was very disappointing to say the least. I felt terrible for all the people whom I had recruited into the company. All of us lost money in this venture, but it did help me realize my own potential, and that was priceless to me. I would never be the same. It was a step toward my independence for the first time in my life.

Chapter 12

Having all six boys in school somewhat freed up my time, but I was still running to school two to three times a day to take some or all of the boys and pick them up or feeding them before sports practices. There were days when I felt overwhelmed, but I wouldn't trade it for the world. This was my responsibility, and I loved it. I loved watching these boys become their own person. Each one had a different personality, and each had their own special gift and talent. I wanted them all to know their unique identities, but more importantly I wanted them to know the Lord Jesus Christ as their personal Lord and Savior. My desire was for them to be godly men, strong in their faith. With that they would make good choices in life.

More and more the thought of beginning a career entered my mind. I started to research the requirements of a nursing career. I knew I would have to complete my high school to get a GED equivalency, so I contacted the high school to begin the process. The thought of doing something for myself seemed exciting but unrealistic. I had conflicting thoughts and feelings about it. At this same time, I kept having reoccurring dreams where I was holding a baby boy in my arms. After having the exact same dream three times, I told my husband, Mark, about it. He looked at me funny and asked, "Are you pregnant?" Of course I wasn't pregnant. I had a tubal ligation after having Luke, so I knew it wasn't that, but what I didn't know at the time was that Mark's sister Wilma was pregnant!

Wilma was a troubled young lady. Very unstable. She ran with the wrong crowd and abused drugs and alcohol. She would leave the Amish community and then she'd go back. We never knew from one visit to the next whether she'd be in street clothes or dressed Amish. She kept getting in trouble with the law and with the Amish church. After approximately eight months Wilma came to us for help. She had been arrested for shoplifting and was sentenced to serve time in jail. The big problem was she was eight months pregnant with no dad in the picture, and she wanted us to keep the baby for her while she served her jail sentence! What a bombshell! What would we do?

I knew deep down we would keep the baby for her. Mark was apprehensive about it. Also I would have to put my plans to go back to school on hold for the time being. But the fact was I just knew he belonged with us, his family. Our six sons would be happy to help care for their little cousin for as long as necessary. And so it was decided. We told Wilma we would keep her baby until she served her jail time.

When it was getting close to the time to deliver the baby, I asked Wilma if she wanted to go shopping for baby clothes, as she hadn't seemed excited to do any of that. And she responded with, "You're going to have him; you choose his clothes." I think I was more excited about this baby than she was. It was heart-wrenching to see her lifestyle of drinking and substance abuse had not changed even during pregnancy. I was very concerned about the damage she might be doing to her baby. So when she finally went into labor, I drove her to the hospital to deliver him. The baby's daddy was not in the picture. Her parents weren't going to be there, so that left me to go and be her support. After a long, painful delivery, a beautiful baby boy was born. As the doctor tried to place the baby on Wilma's stomach like they routinely do, she screamed and pushed him away! The bewildered doctor then looked at me, and I reached for the baby and snuggled him in my arms. I was the mother he bonded with, not knowing at the time that I would be his mother for life.

After being released from the hospital, Wilma, along with baby Jamie, came to our house to stay until she would check into the county correctional facility to serve her sentence. She and little Jamie were with us for two months. In those two months our family had added pressures and responsibilities. It was heart-wrenching to watch this little guy detox from her addictions. This truly is the ultimate form of child abuse—to expose the baby to drugs and alcohol before he is ever born. But we all loved cute little Jamie. He was a joy and a delight. I immediately took him to my then chiropractor (my friend Rica), who also practiced alternative health care. She gave me some great information and direction in helping Jamie detox. We wanted this baby to be as healthy as possible in spite of the exposure to substance abuse. He had no idea what laid in store in his future.

As Wilma served her sentence on work release, I would take Jamie to visit her on her lunch break once a week. Being incarcerated kept Wilma sober and she seemed to enjoy our visits. She was pleasant to be around, and she was a hard worker when she was not under the influence of alcohol and drugs. Because of her good behavior, she was released after serving her sentence for 10 months.

After her release, Wilma settled into an apartment, she kept her job in the factory and I continued to babysit Jamie every day as she worked. It wasn't long until Wilma returned to her old life of drugs and alcohol. Every night she would come and pick up Jamie and take him home only for him to be abused. Wilma threatened to take Jamie and leave the state. It wasn't long before Child Protective Services made a visit to her apartment and decided it was not the best place for Jamie to live. Therefore, Jamie became a ward of the state.

They asked us to keep Jamie, as we were the only family that he really knew and felt safe with. We became his custodial parents. We then had a huge decision to make. Should we ask for adoption? Could we handle that responsibility? I pleaded with Wilma to try to get her to change her ways and to comply with the state. They asked her to attend classes to teach her how to be a better parent. But she refused.

When Jamie turned two years old, we were granted adoption, making Jamie our seventh son. We became his parents for life. This was a bittersweet experience. It was so sad to see the choices Wilma was making. It seemed like such a waste of life. How could she choose drugs and alcohol over a sweet, innocent baby?

Jamie seemed to love his life at our house with us as his family. My six sons enjoyed having Jamie and loved taking him to sports events, where he got all kinds of attention from people. Jamie was a very happy-go-lucky little boy. He loved life so much. One day when Wilma came to visit, he ran toward the stairway and looked back at Wilma and said, "No, Wilma! This is my home!" It seemed as if he felt threatened by her very presence. I tried my best to get through to Wilma. I so needed and wanted her to get her life on track and be a mother to Jamie. I could not make her want something she did not want. Unfortunately, this very sad situation had been brought on by individual choices, and these were the consequences.

Life with all of its challenges at times became overwhelming, but I was learning that I could rely on my heavenly Father totally and completely. I learned so much about Him. I learned that I am never alone. He walks with me every step of the way. Through the hard, fiery trials, He's right there, giving me inspiration, courage and strength. I leaned on Him more and more.

I learned truly to be content in every situation. When I felt alone and frightened, I learned to lean on Jesus and make do and pull from the resources available around me. I learned to gather from what I had in my surroundings. Countless times I found myself thinking about the future. Somehow I knew there was a brighter future. I just knew it deep inside. A future where addictions would no longer control my home or my life.

For now, I would focus on raising my seven sons and be the best mother I could possibly be with the help of God. He tells us in His Word to raise up a child in the way he should go and when he is old he would not depart from it. I often prayed and asked God to be the heavenly Father to my sons since their earthly father was not fulfilling his role. It still brings tears to my eyes when I think of the void left in their hearts by not having a godly example of a father or even a close father-son bond. They would need major healing for such deep soul wounds.

This is where I felt so inadequate and so sorry that I could not provide that for them. My dear, dear sons. They didn't ask to be born into a dysfunctional home. I wouldn't have chosen that for them. They deserved to be loved and taught by example by a father who loved them more than himself. A father who would cherish them and put their needs above his own. A father who loved them more than life itself. How my heart yearned to provide that for my boys, but I could not.

I tried to compensate for that in other ways by surrounding them with godly men and women at church, church functions, and even youth camp. We couldn't financially afford those things, but I did everything in my power to provide this kind of support for them. I did my best to help them excel in sports, and when awards nights came around, I attended alone as if I were a single mom. I couldn't hold back the tears when their coaches would talk about their achievements and describe my sons and their strengths and accomplishments to the crowd. They knew my sons better than their own dad did. I was very thankful for the influence these coaches had on my boys, as well as for the examples and leadership they set forth for my sons. I knew on my own it was impossible to provide all those needs for them, but God knew exactly who to put in their lives for positive direction to help lead and guide them into their destinies. And for that I was grateful.

Their dad did teach them a good work ethic. In the summertime when they didn't have school or sports practice or games, he took them to the job site, where they had hands-on experience and learned the building trade. He also taught them how to hunt wild game at a young age. The two older boys both shot their first deer before the age of 16. We also butchered our own beef and pork, which was a family affair. These were things that we enjoyed as a neighborhood event in the Amish community. Being self-sufficient was a trait I was thankful that they taught us.

Chapter 13

With all of life's twists and turns, I learned to lean on Jesus. I knew He would help us through anything and everything. We had our share of setbacks and illnesses, accidents and hospital visits. With seven sons, there was never a dull moment. They were ornery and rambunctious boys, and also mischievous at times. Ok, I'll admit, they were ornery lots of times. I was thankful to be able to raise them out in the country where they could be free to run and play. They had their three-wheelers and ponies. They loved roaming the woods, where they built forts and tree houses.

They also liked weightlifting, which is what Nathan was doing one night out in the barn when he dropped the bar on his abdomen. He came inside after it happened and told me about it. He seemed ok, but later we saw he had blood in his urine. I was alarmed immediately and took him to the emergency room, where we found out for the first time that he has a horseshoe kidney! This meant he didn't have two normal kidneys; instead, his kidneys were connected at the top. So when he dropped the bar it fell on top of his kidney, and that's what caused it to bleed. The doctor also discovered that his ureter tube was abnormal, which meant surgery was needed to correct it.

This was devastating news for us. Another hospital visit. Another son in surgery! How much of this could I possibly endure? I was tired. Tired of hospital visits. Tired of having to be there alone. Tired of the struggle. When would these situations ever change? Would it always be like this? Would it ever get easier? So many questions and concerns went through my mind as I planned another hospital stay.

I made several trips to the Riley Children's hospital in Indianapolis, Indiana, where Nathan would be having his surgery to correct his kidney. A lot of planning went into this hospital stay. It was two hours from home and he needed to stay for close to a week, which meant I had to find someone willing to come and stay with the rest of the boys. Mark had to work and someone needed to take my place at home. Such an ordeal!

When the day came for Nathan to go into surgery, I was prepared, but that didn't make it any easier to let him go into the operating room alone. He was very nervous, anxious, apprehensive, and all the other emotions that come with these situations. I tried to put up a brave front to keep him calm and we prayed together. We believed God would bring him through the surgery and heal him completely. I waited in the family waiting room where other mothers were sitting. I prayed and watched the clock. I tried to read, but I couldn't focus. I called home to check on the rest of the boys. They were surviving without me. Hour after excruciating hour would drag by. The doctor came out periodically to keep me updated as the surgery progressed.

Finally, after what seemed like many hours, I was told Nathan was now in the recovery room. I breathed a sigh of relief and called Mark to let him know the surgery was done. Now I wanted to see my son. He was very drowsy as the sedation was wearing off, and he looked white as a sheet. I was alarmed, but the doctor reassured me that this was normal and told me what to expect in the days ahead. My dear boy Nathan. Such a traumatic surgery at such a young age!

Slowly but steadily, Nathan began to recover. When he was able to sit in a chair and leave his hospital bed, we would go to the recreation room, where we would join and interact with other families who were in similar situations as us. Meeting new people helped to pass the time until Nathan could be dismissed to go home. He was relieved and happy when he finally got to go back home and be reunited with his brothers.

It wasn't long until life was back to normal and everyone back in school. Everyone except Jamie. Now it was just me and him while the rest were out of the house for the day. Jamie loved the one-on-one interaction. It was obvious he loved his life with us and was a very happy, sweet little boy. He was so cute and caught the attention of many people when we were out and about. I enjoyed having him in our life. I hoped and prayed we could adequately care for him and fulfill his needs in our home despite the brokenness in our divided home.

Many, many nights, long after everyone else went to bed, I would sit in my recliner and let my mind wander back to simpler days. Days when I was a young girl at home with Mom and Dad, before the complications of married life. Before the chaotic, dysfunctional home I lived in now. I'd think about my siblings and wonder, *Where are they now?* I wondered if they had completely forgotten about their oldest sister. If I could live that life one more time, how different things would be. If I had known then what I knew now, I would have stayed there longer, in the security of my parents who loved me.

Those memories brought a flood of tears. The memories of coming downstairs in the morning to the sounds and smells of Mom cooking breakfast. The aroma of coffee brewing in the kettle. The sound and smell of bacon frying in the cast iron skillet on the kerosene stove. Dad sitting by the kitchen table, sipping his coffee and waiting for his driver to pick him up and take him to work. He was a man of few words, especially in the morning. He would talk in short sentences, and if I didn't listen closely, I wasn't sure who he was talking to or what exactly he was saying.

One of the things I loved about my dad was his sense of humor. He loved to tease and make us laugh. I appreciated his laid-back personality and positive attitude. Those were things I missed more than mere words could tell. I missed the simplicity of the seemingly uncomplicated life of the Amish culture.

To me it seemed like life became increasingly difficult. I always felt like I was living in survival mode. The lack of communication or even companionship between my husband and me was unbearable at times. And as the boys grew up into teenagers, the demands became greater. I didn't know how long I could make it through this life. How much stress could a human body physically endure? How long would I last?

I often thought about how much better life could be if I could contribute financially. I would feel less stuck and less worried about how I would feed my family. Having seven sons to clothe and feed cost more money than we seemed to have. There were days when I just didn't know what I would cook for them to eat. Therefore, we ate lots of soups and sandwiches and casseroles. God always provided just enough. I never one time had to put my kids to bed hungry, and for that I was very grateful. But I just could not shake that feeling of helplessness. The feeling of being so stuck. It seemed I lived in survival mode constantly, always wondering how we would make ends meet and keep the family fed. It was a constant struggle. Without God's help, I would've never been able to bear the load.

There were many things I really enjoyed about life as a mom raising seven boys. They were now getting into their teenage years. Sebastian was getting to be more independent as he turned 18, and in his senior year of high school, he went to look for an after-school job. It really helped that he was a strong independent boy who had a huge sense of responsibility. He was determined to become a successful businessman someday. He was more interested in making an income than he was being involved in sports.

He soon found a job at Scott's Grocery Store bagging groceries. He enjoyed the interaction with people and seemed to love his job. Soon after, he also found a summertime job on a hog farm just a couple miles from home. He was an ambitious young man. So responsible. I never had to give him a curfew in his young teen years. He was always respectful and obedient. I didn't see the teenage rebellion I had heard parents talk about before. I was extremely proud of him. Now, as an adult, he was a huge help to me. He also helped me so much with Jamie. He was so adorable, and Sebastian would take him to the football games where all their friends flocked around him and lavished their attention on the cute little guy.

I was relieved to finally have custody and get Jamie out of harm's way. But all of the paperwork and meetings and doctor's visits were overwhelming. And then there were the court sessions we had to attend. The State versus Wilma. I so much wanted Wilma to go into therapy and restructure her life in order to become a better parent and be a part of Jamie's life. There were days when I thought that's what she wanted, too. She would say all the right things, but she would not follow through. It was a long, drawn-out process, but finally the state granted the adoption. Other than the stress of dealing with the legal consequences, we loved having Jamie. He was a delight to have. There was an eight-and-a-half-year gap between my youngest biological son, Luke, and Jamie, so it was like starting a new family all over again. It was a huge adjustment for all of us and a sacrifice as well. But I was happy to adopt Jamie as my son rather than allow the state to put him into a home where everyone was a stranger. I could not bear the thought of that.

Chapter 14

It was a warm morning in the middle of summertime. I was sitting on the porch, drinking my morning coffee and enjoying the sunrise and the warm, soft breeze blowing into my face. I loved that feeling. I watched as the hummingbirds flitted about, trying to get to the sweet nectar at the feeders. I marveled at God's creation and wondered how He ever created such magnificent, tiny birds and the speed of their little wings and their bright colors. It seemed at that moment all was well with the world.

I was basking in that peaceful moment, which was short lived as my mind started to think about the day ahead of me. It would be a very uncomfortable day—the day one of my brothers would be getting married. I was given permission to attend the Amish wedding, but they would not allow me to be a part of the family functions. I was simply granted the privilege of attending the wedding, but I would have to sit off at a table of strangers, who had never joined the Amish church, to eat the meal they served. This was because of the shunning! I guess I should have been grateful to be able to be there at all. But I felt like I was on the outside just watching the whole event. It seemed surreal. Jamie was the only one who came with me. It was too uncomfortable for Mark to come with me, and the boys were getting older and were not willing to subject themselves to the shunning. It did not make any sense to them; they did not understand why we had to be treated differently than any of their cousins.

It was this exact painful situation they had experienced too many times and they didn't like it. I can't say I blamed them. It was very painful. But I was not about to miss out on my brother's wedding. I chose to endure the pain of being shunned over the pain of missing the wedding, and so I took little Jamie and we went for a little while. I felt extremely uncomfortable. I encountered people I had not seen in ages. Some of them were as friendly as they were allowed to be, and some of them refused to speak to me at all.

Taking in the activities of the day brought back many memories of my own Amish wedding. All the hustle and bustle. Seemed like a hundred people just to prepare and serve the food. It was not just ordinary food; it was an Amish wedding meal which consisted of home-cooked foods such as pies, cakes, tapioca or date pudding, and, of course, the thin sugary crusts called Knee Patches. The main course at Amish weddings would typically include fried or grilled chicken, mashed potatoes, dressing and gravy, fresh corn or mixed vegetables, buttered noodles and a salad. Just talking about an Amish wedding meal makes me hungry still to this day. The Amish can cook some of the best-tasting food in the world. The meal at the wedding this day was no exception.

Little Jamie sat quietly beside me, eating his food, oblivious to the discomfort of the shunning. He was too young to realize what was happening. For the most part everyone who had joined us at this table was pretty quiet. At times, it became awkwardly quiet. After the meal, I made my way through the crowded room to reach the wedding corner where the bride and groom were sitting with their witnesses. My brother smiled and extended his hand to shake mine. I congratulated both him and his new bride and left as soon as I could, hoping my feelings of discomfort weren't too obvious. I breathed a huge sigh of relief as I buckled Jamie into his seat. I kissed his sweet smiling face. He didn't realize the comfort he provided just by being with me.

The pain of rejection is so excruciating. It makes a person appreciate kindness in a big way. I prayed, *Lord help me to always be kind. Help me to never inflict pain and judgment by shunning others and pushing them away.* According to the KJV version of the Bible, shunning is the exact opposite of what the Word commands of us. It tells us to love, not hate and reject. Living according to scripture is abiding by the Golden Rule.

And that is the motto I follow. And hopefully, I instilled it into my children as well.

One of the things Mark liked to do with our sons was deer hunting. And the boys loved hunting just as much as he did. Sebastian wanted to shoot a deer so badly. One day, when he was sitting out in a tree stand, he asked God to give him a deer. He thought it would be a good idea to make a deal with God. He started talking to Him and promised that if he could shoot a deer, he would go to church more often. Sebastian couldn't believe his eyes when he saw a deer come running. As he lifted his loaded gun and shot at it, the deer ran towards the woods. Sebastian shot the gun a few more times as he watched the deer disappear, then ran in the direction he saw the deer go. At his surprise, there it lay. He had gotten his first deer! From then on, Sebastian kept his promise and went to church faithfully.

He made lots of friends at the church. Two young men he was especially close to were the Loker twins. He enjoyed their company and they became very close until the twins and their families moved to another state. Sebastian missed them immensely. He continued to go to church and became very active in the youth group. He and his brothers enjoyed going to summer Bible camp where they learned a lot and seemed to be growing spiritually and wanted to serve God. It was very encouraging to see their interest in the things of God at this young age. It gave me hope that the struggles of leaving the Amish community were not in vain.

When October came around and it was Sebastian's 16th birthday, I decided to surprise him. I invited the Loker twins to come and celebrate his 16th birthday. I told them that I would pay for the plane tickets, and they were happy to accept the invitation. We were all very excited as the time drew closer and we had all the details planned out for the surprise birthday party.

Mark agreed to take Sebastian away for a few hours and spend some one-on-one time with him, which was a delight to Sebastian. This would be a moment that Sebastian would cherish forever. He or his brothers rarely had their dad's undivided attention, which they craved and needed. So, this was a double blessing for Sebastian. He got to spend some much needed one-on-one time with his dad and a birthday surprise.

I will never forget the look of surprise and happiness on Sebastian's face when he came home and saw that his friends had flown in from out of state to celebrate his 16th birthday with him. This was a fun time that would never be forgotten. It gave me great pleasure to see him so happy. The twins were happy to see Sebastian as well. They stayed up and celebrated long into the night, catching up on each other's lives and all that had happened since the twins moved away.

There were many happy times raising a family of boys. Even though I so much wanted a daughter, I couldn't have asked for more happiness than we had with seven sons. There was never a dull moment. The fun, rough and tumble days we experienced created memories for a lifetime. My babysitter Rachel can vouch for that.

When the boys were younger and I needed someone to help out with the boys, or when I had to leave for a few hours, she was always willing to come and stay with them. She had to be tough as nails. She was the only person that could stay with Luke. He refused to stay with anyone else. I was very grateful for Rachel's help. I often felt like she was a godsend. I never had to hire babysitters when we were still Amish because back then we had brothers and sisters, grandparents, aunts and uncles, a whole community of relatives helping each other with not only babysitting, but everything else.

The summertime memories were my favorites. My son Luke loved to go mudding on our little garden tractor along with one of his buddies. I will never forget when they came back from just such an adventure.

Luke and his buddy, each one on their own little garden tractors, came back from playing in the woods, both covered in mud from top to bottom, including the tractors! What a sight to see. All I could see was their eyes and their smiles of delight. The rest of their bodies were covered in mud. I might add they didn't come into the house to get cleaned up. They used the garden hose to wash off the mud.

There were scary times as well, like the time when Alex and his dad were riding together on a three-wheeler, speeding through an open field, when they hit a deep hole they didn't see. They were both thrown off and knocked out. Somehow, they found their way back home, still dazed. In my opinion, they should've gotten medical attention, but they would not hear any of it. Such adventurous and scary times.

The boys all had friends that would come home from school with them. Some of them became like part of the family. They seemed more like my sons than friends. They loved the rough and tumble country life where they wrestled, played football, rode four-wheelers and hung out in the kitchen where it seemed like I was forever cooking food or doing dishes. But they seemed to be content to eat whatever food I cooked for my boys which was a lot of soups, sandwiches, or casseroles. They soon learned what Amish cooking was all about and they seemed to enjoy eating it. We were blessed and surrounded with really good kids. For that I am forever grateful.

The years seemed to fly by so quickly. One after the other the boys turned 16, 17, then 18. One right after the other, they were getting their driver's licenses and jobs which gave them some independence and gave me some much-needed time to do some paint jobs for extra cash. I actually started my own interior and exterior painting business. I would take a couple of the boys with me and we would blast old paint off of barns and apply new paint. I would climb up the ladder with the boys and work alongside them painting apartment buildings, houses and such. This is where I found some self-worth. I learned that I could do more than just cook and clean and keep house and raise boys. It gave me a new lease on life. I saw that I could create an income for myself, which gave me some much-needed confidence. I had inherited my dad's "do whatever it takes to get the job done" attitude. Working very hard was a way of life for me, which I actually enjoyed. I loved the sense of accomplishment. It helped me feel fulfilled.

Along with having their own driver's licenses and gaining independence came the dangers of teenage drivers. This gave me many sleepless nights, such as the night when Wyatt and Alex were out late with their friends. It was snowing and the roads were slick. Wyatt was driving through a small town where there were two ponds side by side. He must've been going too fast. His car started sliding. He couldn't stop and drove up to the very edge of the pond so that the front of the car was actually in the water.

Being frightened, they decided not to call the police officers. Instead they found another way home. I didn't learn of any of this until the next morning. I was getting ready to go to church. Wyatt and Alex decided they couldn't go with me since they needed to fish their car out of the pond. I did not realize the extent of the danger until I got to church and a friend of mine told me he saw the car in the pond. Not knowing whose car it was, he told his wife that whoever was in that car had a guardian angel watching over them.

To this day, I believe that's what saved the lives of my two ornery boys. The protection of the angels. We didn't have a lot of material possessions, but that did not stop my boys from living life to the fullest. Every one of them seemed to have a healthy outlook on life, driven to be all that they could be. I did my best to instill in them that they each have the ability to become all they ever dreamed of. Like it tells us in Philippians 4:13, "I can do all things through Christ which strengthens me." To this day, I believe God worked in and through them. There were many accomplishments, like the time their small three-star school won a football game against a large five-star school.

 The boys were a little nervous about this game. I reminded them of the David versus Goliath story in the bible. Lo and behold, our little three-star school won the game to everyone's surprise. The next day there was a write up in the local newspaper. In the article they stated, "This was truly a David versus Goliath game." What a confirmation to my young boys' hearts. It also boosted my faith in my Lord. I knew even then that He is looking out for my family.

Watching the boys compete in sports was a joy to me. Growing up in the Amish community I didn't have the privilege of competing in sports against other schools or look forward to going to state and competing against the best of the best teams. It made me extremely happy that my boys got to experience that privilege. It was a very proud mama moment when their name was added in the *Gridiron Greats* book as some of the top athletes.

Then there was the time when Alex went to state with his wrestling team. He was a very tough wrestler. Wrestling is a rough contact sport. It always made me nervous to watch my boys compete in it. When Alex went to state, I was there with him. I hurt and was proud at the same time when Alex refused to stop wrestling because of a dislocated shoulder. They simply wrapped duct tape around his shoulder and he kept right on wrestling. I still don't know how he did it. It hurt me just to watch him. His determination and perseverance were out of this world.

All throughout their lives I could see the hand of God on my boys. And there were many, many situations when it would have been a disaster if it had not been for the hand of God on them, like the time when Wyatt was driving his black Grand Am. He had left the house a few minutes earlier when we received a phone call. Mark answered the phone and I overheard the conversation.

He said, "What? Wyatt hit a semi?"

My heart sank. My first question was, "Which hospital did they take him to?"

A million questions raced through my mind. *Is he still alive? Will I get to talk to him? Will he ever be ok again?*

After Mark got all of the information, we learned that he was still at the scene of the accident which was about 10 minutes from our house. We rushed to his side to find him standing by his car. The driver of the semi-truck was someone that we knew and he was telling us that he decided at the last minute to take the truck that was lower to the ground. If he would have been driving his semi-truck that was higher up Wyatt would have gone underneath the semi-truck and would have been killed instantly. He'd wrecked his car but he was alive and refused treatment. He was shaken up, but he was not hurt. He admitted that he was driving too fast and was distracted while trying to find the music he wanted to hear on his radio. I breathed a deep sigh of relief to see he was going to be okay. This would be a hard lesson, but hopefully he would learn from it. Once again, I had to say, "Thank you, Jesus, for your protecting hand."

My boys were growing up fast. I had mixed emotions about that. I was happy to see they were finding their way in life despite their dysfunctional home. Sebastian was the first-born with a huge sense of responsibility for his siblings. He was the trailblazer. Not only did he have the obstacles of the chaotic home life, but at the same time juggling school, work, sports and church, trying to find his niche. He wanted so much to be a part of his Amish cousins' lives.

Since he had never been a member of the Amish church, it was permitted for him to visit with them. Since he had his drivers license, he would sometimes take them places. He enjoyed these times immensely. It didn't seem fair to him or myself that he had to be separated from his own relatives because of my decision to leave the

Amish community and follow Christ as I felt led to do. I hoped that someday he and his brothers would understand my decision to leave the Amish church and follow Christ was extremely hard, but necessary, no matter how painful it was at the time.

When I think about all that transpired since leaving my Amish world, I am convinced we did the right thing. Watching the boys grow up into young adults with each of their personalities developing from toddlers to school age boys and on into adulthood, along with the failures, the victories and successes. The times when each one individually discovered their place in Christ by confession of their faith in Christ and His shed blood on the cross, followed by water baptism. That major life changing decision was the absolute most important decision they would ever make in this life. Watching all these changes helped me to know without a doubt we did the right thing by leaving the Amish community and teaching them that salvation cannot be earned. It is not based on what we wear or on works, period. It is a born-again experience. Accepting the fact that Jesus took our sins upon himself and willingly died on the cross in our place. There is nothing we can do to add to that. If we try, it's like we are saying that the suffering and dying on the cross was not enough. To me, His sacrifice is enough and I accept it and say thank you a million times over.

I am forever grateful for what Jesus did on the cross for a wretched sinner such as I. My seven sons all grew up into young men that I am extremely proud of. They all became independent young men. Each one choosing a profession to be proud of.

I could write a book on each one of their paths in life, their choices in spouses, friends, careers, victories and successes. I dearly love my sons and would be willing to do it all over again. Even the hardships and sacrifices, the tough choices. It was worth it all. I will say so long until the next book where this story continues...

Printed in Great Britain
by Amazon